How To Get Your Kids To Go To Bed

How To Get Your Kids To Go To Bed

Lights Out. No Fight. You Won.

The Manual

Julene and George Gervais

Focus On It, LLC

Focus On It, LLC
P.O. Box 472
Cumberland Center, ME 04021

Published by Focus On It, LLC North Yarmouth, ME
HowToGetYourKidsToGotoBed.com

Digital Edition ISBN: 979-8-9927884-1-9
Paperback Edition ISBN: 979-8-9927884-4-0

Also available in audio edition.

Cover designed by George Gervais

To our kids — who have taught us the wonders of the world through their eyes, their laughter, their learning, their wonderment, and their love.

Oh, and their cooking and IT skills.

CONTENTS

Preface:
Why This Actually Matters

Here is something nobody tells you at the pediatrician's office, in the parenting books, or in the well-meaning advice dispensed at school pickup:

Sleep is not a parenting nicety. It is not the reward at the end of a good evening. It is not something your child will eventually figure out on their own if you just stop worrying about it.

Sleep is the thing.

While your child sleeps, their brain consolidates everything they learned that day — the math, the social cues, the emotional processing, the physical skills. Their immune system does its most aggressive repair work. Their growth hormone peaks. The neural connections that will define how they think, regulate emotion, and engage with the world are being pruned and strengthened in ways that cannot happen any other way, at any other time. There is no supplement, no enrichment program, no extra tutoring session that does what eight to ten hours of quality sleep does for a developing brain.

The research is not subtle about the consequences of getting this wrong. Children who are chronically under-slept are more impulsive, more emotionally reactive, more likely to struggle with attention and learning, more susceptible to illness, and — by adolescence — more vulnerable to anxiety and depression than their well-rested peers. The effects compound quietly over months and years, in ways that rarely get traced back to their source.

The child who learns to sleep well is being handed an advantage that will follow them for decades. Better focus. Better emotional regulation. Better health. Better performance at everything they try — school, sports, relationships, work. You are not just trying to get through tonight. You are building something.

We wrote this book because we were failing at bedtime in our own house — spectacularly, repeatedly, and in ways that will become apparent very quickly once you start reading. We are not sleep researchers or child psychologists. We are parents of three kids — ages nine, fourteen, and twenty-one — who got tired of losing the same battle every night and went looking for answers that actually worked in a real house with real children and a real amount of parental energy.

What follows is what we found. Funny where it deserves to be funny. Honest where honesty is more useful than reassurance (sometimes embarrassingly so). And practical in a way that starts tonight, not someday.

Your kid can sleep. You can get there. Let's keep going.

— George & Julene Gervais, Authors and Parents, just like you.

Chapter 1:

Why Bedtime Is a War
(And Why Smart Parents Keep Losing It)

We had a plan.

It wasn't a complicated plan. It wasn't a *good* plan, exactly, but it was a plan, and we committed to it with the full confidence of two parents who have been at this long enough to know better and are doing it anyway.

Twenty minutes.

Just twenty minutes of iPad. Tomorrow morning Julene's on a plane. First thing. The National Corporate Sales meeting — the one where everyone ends up on stage at some point, doing role-plays, displaying exactly how prepared they are. Or aren't. In front of peers. In front of people from other districts she's never met. In front of her boss. In front of the President of the company.

Julene needs to be prepared. She needs twenty uninterrupted minutes to finish getting there. And Juney is right there, and the iPad is right there, and twenty minutes is *nothing.* Twenty minutes is fine.

Julene hands over the iPad with the quiet, slightly guilty efficiency of a bank teller who knows the guy on the other side of the counter is about to rob the place.

"Just twenty minutes," she says. "Then it's bedtime."

Our daughter doesn't even look up.

Julene sits down. She opens her laptop. She actually gains *focus* — legitimately, productively, beautifully focused — and she gets the work done, and it feels amazing, and she closes the laptop and looks up and —

It is 11:17pm.

The iPad is still going. Juney is horizontal on the couch, glassy-eyed, wrapped in a blanket she definitely got herself, surrounded by evidence of a snack nobody authorized. She has the look of someone who has been watching YouTube for so long that she has forgotten her own name.

And we think: *How.*

Then George walks in the room in his underwear. He came down after going to the bathroom and noticing that Juney wasn't in her bed.

"What the......?!"

He looked at his daughter. He looked at the iPad. He looked at the time.

"What are you doing?! The morning is going to be impossible!"

Juney's eyes welled up immediately — the specific tears that are designed, with surgical precision, to disarm a parent before they can finish the thought they were having. George recognized them for exactly what they were.

He was disarmed anyway. He has never fully solved this problem.

This is the story of bedtime. Not the version in the parenting books — and NOT the version where the parent calmly dims the lights at 7:30 and reads *Goodnight Moon* while lavender diffuses gently into the air and the child sighs contentedly and drifts off to sleep like a person in a mattress commercial.

Like you, we deal with the real version. The one where you lose ninety minutes you didn't have, your kid is now *more* awake than when you started, and the bedtime conversation — which you are now having at 11:17pm with a child who has had too much screen and not enough dinner — is technically a hostage negotiation.

You are a good parent. You are a tired parent. And somehow, *every single night*, bedtime turns into a thing.

Why?

That is actually the right question, and most parents never stop long enough to ask it, because they are too busy in the middle of the thing to think about why the thing keeps happening. So let's ask it. Why is bedtime a war? Why do smart, loving, capable adults — people who manage teams and run households and remember to pay the car insurance — consistently lose a battle of wills to someone who still occasionally puts their shoes on the wrong feet?

Here's the honest answer: *because everything about the modern evening is working against you.*

The Setup Is Rigged

Think about what the average family evening actually looks like.

You get home later than you meant to. Dinner is later than it should be, which means the kitchen gets cleaned up later, which means whatever wind-down time you were planning for has quietly evaporated. Someone has homework that they didn't mention until 8pm. Someone else needs to be driven somewhere, or picked up from somewhere, or is upset about something that happened at school that you're only now hearing about. The dog needs to go out. There are dishes.

And underneath all of this is a child — or two, or three — who has been *on* all day. School, activity, stimulation, social stress, screen time in the car, more screens after school, a snack, an argument, more screens. Their nervous system has been pinging like a pinball machine since 7am.

And now you need them to *stop.*

Just... stop. Turn off the lights in that pinball machine. Lie down. Close their eyes. Be unconscious.

On *command.*

The fact that this works at all, on any night, is actually remarkable when you say it out loud. You are asking a small human being — whose brain is still *literally under construction* — to perform one of the most neurologically complex feats a person can perform: voluntarily transitioning from full alertness to sleep, on a schedule, in response to an external instruction.

Adults can barely do this. We have wine for this.

Why You Keep Losing

Here's the thing nobody says plainly enough: the bedtime battle isn't mostly about your kid. It's about the setup.

When bedtime goes wrong — and it goes wrong in the same ways, in the same order, in houses all over the world — it's almost never because your child is uniquely defiant, or because you're doing something uniquely wrong. It's because a predictable set of conditions produces a predictable result, and those conditions were set in motion hours before anybody said the word "bedtime."

The iPad at 8pm wasn't a parenting failure. It was a rational decision made by an exhausted person who needed twenty minutes and used the tool that was available. The fact that it turned into ninety minutes isn't a character flaw. It's physics. You set a ball rolling down a hill and then were surprised when it reached the bottom.

Most bedtime problems trace back to one of four things:

Timing. Bedtime got pushed later than the kid's biology wants it to be, and now you're fighting against a second wind that shouldn't exist.

Stimulation. Something in the last hour — a screen, a rough-housing session with Dad, a snack with enough sugar to power a small city — lit up your child's nervous system right when it needed to be dimming.

Inconsistency. The rules shifted, or they shifted yesterday, or they've shifted enough times that your kid now understands — correctly — that the rules are negotiable. Smart kids are very good at identifying negotiable rules. Yours is probably smart.

Your own tank. You are tired. You are depleted. You have been making decisions since 6am and your willpower is a husk. On a full tank, you could hold the line. On this tank, you're going to cave somewhere between "one more chapter" and "can you just lay down with me for a little while."

None of this is a verdict on you. It is a map of the terrain. And once you know the terrain, you can stop fighting the battle you keep losing and start winning a different one.

What This Book Is

This is not a book that will judge you for the iPad thing. You should know that upfront.

It is also not a book that will give you a perfect bedtime routine that works the first night and every night thereafter, because that book would be lying to you and you deserve better.

What this book will do is explain what's actually happening — in your kid's body, in your house, in your own exhausted decision-making — and then give you specific, realistic things to try. Starting tonight if you want. Or starting Thursday. No pressure. We're all just doing our best out here at 10pm.

By the end, you'll have a routine that's actually buildable in a real house with real children and a real amount of parental energy, a clear-eyed understanding of the things that are secretly sabotaging you, and a one-page cheat sheet you can save to your phone for the nights when you can't remember any of this.

But first: the biology. Because it turns out there's a very good reason your kid got a second wind the second you said "time for bed." And once you understand it, you'll never look at an 8pm iPad session the same way again.

Chapter 2:

What's Actually Happening in That Little Body at 8pm

You are not a scientist.

You don't need to be. But somewhere between the iPad incident and the 1:30am cheeseburger (more on that later), you deserve to know that there is actual biology underneath all of this — real, documented, peer-reviewed science that explains why your kid gets a second wind the exact moment you say "time for bed," why your teenager is genuinely nocturnal, and why the harder you push some nights, the more awake everyone gets.

This is not a long chapter. There is no quiz. But by the end of it, at least three things that have been driving you crazy will suddenly make complete sense. And that feeling — the ***"oh THAT'S why"*** feeling — is worth eight minutes of your life.

Let's go.

The Sleep Pressure System (Or: Why Timing Is Everything)

Your child's brain runs two separate systems that work together to produce sleep. Think of them as two dials that both need to be turned up at the same time.

Dial One is called sleep pressure.

From the moment your kid wakes up in the morning, a chemical called adenosine starts building up in their brain. All day long, it accumulates — quietly, steadily — like water filling a tank. The fuller the tank, the sleepier the child. By a certain point in the evening, that tank should be pretty close to full, and the child should be genuinely, organically ready to sleep.

Should be.

Here's the problem: caffeine blocks adenosine. You know this, because caffeine does the same thing for you — it's literally just an adenosine blocker, which is why coffee makes you feel less tired. But your kid isn't drinking coffee.

Except — are they drinking soda? Iced tea? The chocolate milk at school that has more sugar than a Snickers? Some of these have real caffeine loads. And even without caffeine, **sugar creates a temporary adenosine disruption** that looks a lot like a second wind. That 8pm snack you let slide? That's sleep pressure leaking out of the tank right when you needed it full.

"Oh THAT'S why."

Dial Two is melatonin.

Melatonin is the hormone that tells your child's brain: *it's dark, it's time, begin the shutdown sequence.* It's produced by a tiny gland in the brain that is exquisitely, almost comically sensitive to light. Specifically, to blue light — the short-wavelength light that signals to your prehistoric brain that it is the middle of a sunny afternoon and you should be hunting something, not sleeping.

You know what produces an enormous amount of blue light?

Every screen in your house.

The iPad your daughter was watching for twenty minutes — or ninety minutes. The phone your teenager had under his blanket. The TV in the background while you cleaned up after dinner. Every one of those screens was quietly sending a signal to your child's melatonin system that said: *not yet. It's still daytime. Stay up.*

And the melatonin system believed it. Because it's not smart. It's just a light detector, doing its job, completely fooled by a device that fits in a six-year-old's hands.

This is why screens before bed aren't just a "bad habit." They are chemically, neurologically, physically delaying the onset of sleep. Every night you allow screens in the last hour before bed, you are pushing your child's natural sleep onset back — in some studies, by as much as an hour to ninety minutes.

When we first read about this — really understood it, not just nodded past it — George looked up and said: *"Did you know this? No wonder we struggle. We need a new plan."*

Julene put her phone down.

"I told you this. Remember that night I was reading an article at 11pm? On my phone? In bed?"

The irony was not lost on either of them. They were having the blue-light conversation on blue-light devices, at the exact hour blue light does its worst work. This is parenthood. You learn the right thing at the wrong time, on the wrong device, and you do your best with it anyway.

"Oh THAT'S why."

The Cortisol Problem (Or: Why Bedtime Fights Make Everything Worse)

Here's the one that's going to sting a little.

Cortisol is your stress hormone. When something stressful happens — an argument, a raised voice, a high-stakes negotiation about whether teeth actually need to be brushed tonight — cortisol spikes. In adults and children alike. It's a survival response. Your brain thinks there might be a threat, so it starts waking the body up. Heart rate up. Alertness up. Sleep: postponed.

Now think about what bedtime looks like in a lot of houses.

There's a demand. There's resistance. The demand is repeated, louder. There's negotiation. There's a consequence threatened. Someone cries. Someone slams a door. Someone — the parent — says something they slightly regret and then feels guilty about it at 11pm.

Every escalation in that sequence is a cortisol hit. For the kid *and* for you. You are both, physiologically, becoming more awake as the fight progresses.

Here is what this looks like in a real house.

One of us trying to recover from the day. The other trying to get one more thing done before the day ends — even though, by any honest measure, the day has already ended. And then: two kids at the bottom of the stairs. One says *"I can't sleep."* The other — and you already know which one — says *"I'm hungry."*

George loses it. Not dramatically. Not his finest moment, but not a scene either. Just a man who has reached the end of his available patience and let a small amount of it show.

Then Julene loses it. Probably triggered by George, though she would say independently triggered, and she is not wrong.

Two adults, cortisol spiking. Two kids, cortisol spiking. Everyone standing in a hallway at 10pm becoming more awake by the second. This is the opposite of what was supposed to be happening. This is the science, working exactly as described, in our house, on a Tuesday.

The harder you push, the more alert the child becomes. You are accidentally doing the opposite of what you're trying to do.

This is not an argument for never having rules or never holding the line. It's an argument for understanding that *how* you do bedtime is part of the sleep equation — not just *when.* A calm, boring, predictable bedtime produces sleep. A dramatic, high-conflict bedtime produces more cortisol and then a child lying in bed staring at the ceiling wondering if you're still mad at them.

"Oh THAT'S why."

The Teenager Is a Different Animal

Now. Patrick.

Patrick, who we found in our kitchen at 1:30am, standing at the stove in the dark, making himself a cheeseburger and a milkshake, apparently completely unbothered by the fact that he has a math test in approximately six hours. (Be patient! The story is coming, we promise)

Here is what you need to know about Patrick's brain:

At some point between the ages of roughly ten and thirteen, the human brain undergoes a fundamental shift in its circadian rhythm. The internal clock — the one that governs when melatonin releases, when sleep pressure peaks, when the body wants to be asleep and when it wants to be awake — shifts *later.* Not by fifteen minutes. Not by half an hour.

By one to three hours.

This is not a choice. It is not attitude. It is not a phase he'll grow out of quickly. It is a documented, universal, biological feature of adolescent development. Researchers call it "sleep phase delay," and it affects virtually every teenager on earth, across every culture studied. Your teenager's brain is genuinely, chemically programmed to fall asleep later and wake up later than it did when he was eight.

Your kid was not in your kitchen at 1:30am because he was being defiant. He was in your kitchen at 1:30am because his melatonin didn't start rising until 11pm. He wasn't tired. He hadn't been tired for hours. He was hungry, he was awake, and he made the only logical decision available to him: a cheeseburger.

Does this mean you just accept it and let teenagers stay up until 2am? No. We'll get to the reset strategy for teens in Chapter 7. But it does mean that treating a teenager's late sleep schedule exactly like a young child's sleep resistance is going to produce frustration for everyone, because they are genuinely different problems.

A seven-year-old fighting bedtime at 8pm is usually overstimulated and under-routined.

A thirteen-year-old who can't fall asleep until midnight is usually biologically shifted and needs a different intervention entirely.

Same house. Same battle. Different war.

The One-Paragraph Summary You Can Actually Remember

Your kid's brain needs two things to fall asleep: a full adenosine tank (built up over the day, not drained by sugar or caffeine) and a melatonin signal that says *it's dark, it's time* (which screens are actively blocking). Stress and conflict raise cortisol, which fights both of those systems. And if your kid is a teenager, their entire clock has shifted later, which means early bedtimes feel to them the way 3pm feels to you — just not tired yet.

That's it. That's the science.

Everything in the rest of this book — the routine, the reset, the age-specific strategies — is just the practical application of those four things. Now that you know *why,* the *what* is going to make a lot more sense.

But Wait — What About the Kid Who's Tired But Still Won't Sleep?

This one comes up constantly, so let's address it here before we move on.

Your kid is yawning. They're rubbing their eyes. They're doing that glazed, stumbling thing where they walk into a doorframe because their depth perception is going offline. They are *clearly* exhausted. And yet.

The moment you say "okay, bedtime" — they wake up.

What is happening?

Two things, usually working together.

First: you may have missed the window. Sleep pressure and melatonin align to create an optimal sleep window — a period of maybe thirty to forty-five minutes where everything is lined up and falling asleep is relatively easy. Miss that window, and the body assumes something went wrong and course-corrects with a small alertness boost. It's a survival mechanism. The yawning, glazed child you had at 8pm will be a surprisingly animated child at 8:20pm if you didn't catch them in time.

Second: the announcement itself triggers arousal. Saying "time for bed" is, from your child's perspective, a social event. Their brain perks up — *something's happening* — which is exactly the wrong direction. This is one of the reasons a *routine* beats an *announcement* every time. When the same sequence of events happens in the same order every night, the brain starts associating those events with sleep — and begins the shutdown process automatically, without needing to be told. It's Pavlov's bedtime.

We'll build that routine in Chapter 4.

First, Chapter 3 — because before we get to solutions, we need to be honest about the fact that a four-year-old and a thirteen-year-old are not the same problem, do not have the same brain, and absolutely should not have the same bedtime strategy.

Even if they're in the same house.

Even if they share a wall.

Even if one of them just woke you up at 1:30am to inform you, via cheeseburger, that the night is young.

Chapter 3:

The Age Problem — Because a 4-Year-Old and a 13-Year-Old Are Not the Same Disaster

---

Let's establish something immediately.

If you have ever read a parenting book that gave you a bedtime strategy — a real, specific, *this is what you do* strategy — and then tried to apply it to your child and had it fail completely, there is a reasonable chance it didn't fail because you did it wrong.

It failed because it was written for a different age child than the one you have.

Bedtime advice is almost always written for a vague, generic child of unspecified age who behaves in a vague, generic way. But children are not vague or generic. They are alarmingly specific. And what works at four years old not only doesn't work at nine — it will make things actively worse. What works at nine becomes laughable at twelve. And what works at twelve requires an entirely different understanding of what's happening neurologically than what you needed at four.

This chapter is a quick map of the territory. Three buckets. Real behavior. Real reasons. And a preview of the strategies we'll build out in Chapter 4.

Bucket One: The Little Ones (Ages 2–5)

What it looks like

It is 7:45pm. You have done everything right. Bath. Pajamas. The book — *the same book they've requested every night for six weeks, the one you can now recite from memory in a slightly dead voice while thinking about something else entirely.* You turn off the light. You say goodnight. You close the door.

You make it four steps down the hall.

"Mommy."

You stop.

"Mommy."

You do not respond. You have read that you should not respond. You are implementing a strategy.

"MOMMY."

"What."

"I need water."

You get the water. You deliver the water. You close the door again. You make it six steps this time. Progress.

"Daddy."

"What."

"I forgot to tell you something."

"What did you forget to tell me."

"I love you."

And there it is. The kill shot. The thing they know — they absolutely know — you cannot walk away from without responding. You are being emotionally manipulated by someone who still needs help with buttons.

What's actually happening

Children in this age range are not fighting sleep because they're not tired. They are almost always tired. What they are fighting is *separation.*

This is the age of object permanence consolidating, attachment systems firing on all cylinders, and a brain that is genuinely, non-dramatically uncertain about whether the people it loves will still exist in the morning. The "I need water" and the "I love you" and the seventeen other delay tactics are not strategic. They are anxious. The child is buying time with the one currency they have, which is your attention, because your attention is the thing that makes them feel safe.

This doesn't mean you give them unlimited access to your attention at 8pm forever. It means the solution is **safety and predictability**, not firmness and distance. A child who feels securely anchored at bedtime — who knows exactly what happens next, who trusts the routine because it has happened the same way enough times — separates more easily than a child who is trying to read the room and figure out tonight's rules.

The other thing happening at this age: **overtiredness looks like energy.** A two or three-year-old who has blown past their sleep window doesn't get quieter. They get *louder.* More physical. More emotional. More likely to dissolve into tears over something cosmically unfair, like the fact that their crackers broke. If your toddler is bouncing off the walls at 8pm, the answer is almost never "they're not tired yet." It's almost always "they were tired ninety minutes ago and now cortisol has taken over the vehicle."

What this age needs

- **An early, consistent window.** Most children in this range have an optimal sleep onset between 7pm and 8pm. Not 8:30. Not 9. Earlier than you think.

- **The same sequence, every night, no exceptions.** Bath, book, song, light off — or whatever your version is. The sequence *is* the signal. The brain learns to start shutting down when the sequence begins.
- **A bridge object.** A stuffed animal, a nightlight, a specific blanket. Something that stays when you leave. You are giving them a physical anchor for the safety feeling you're walking out the door with.
- **One sanctioned callback.** Give them one. *"I'm going to check on you in five minutes."* Then actually do it. This preempts fourteen unsanctioned callbacks, because the uncertainty — *will they come back?* — is what drives the behavior.

Bucket Two: The School-Age Kid (Ages 6–10)

What it looks like

Your eight-year-old has been told it's bedtime. He has acknowledged this information. He has, in fact, said "okay" — which you have learned means nothing.

Fifteen minutes later you walk past his room and the light is on and he is sitting on the floor surrounded by Lego, assembling something complicated, wearing an expression of profound concentration, as if time itself does not apply to him.

"I thought I said bedtime."

"I know. I just needed to finish this one part."

"You said that twenty minutes ago."

"I know. But then I found this other piece."

He holds up a small yellow brick with the quiet dignity of an archaeologist who has just discovered something significant.

You stand there in the doorway. You are tired. He is not. This is the fundamental injustice of parenthood.

What's actually happening

The school-age child has two things going on that the toddler doesn't.

First: **they have genuinely interesting things to do.** Lego. Books. Art projects. Games. A rich inner world that does not punch out at 8pm just because you'd like it to. The resistance at this age is often less about separation anxiety and more about *opportunity cost.* Going to sleep means stopping something interesting. The ceiling is less compelling than the Lego. This is not defiance. It is completely rational. It is also completely unsustainable, and left unchecked it becomes the pattern that defines the next five years of your evenings.

Second: **they have discovered negotiation.** The toddler delays with emotion. The school-age child delays with *logic.* They will construct arguments. They will identify inconsistencies in your position. They will cite precedent — *"but last Tuesday you let me stay up until nine-thirty"* — with the precision of a small attorney who has been building a case file.

This age group is also where **screens become a serious variable** for the first time. The toddler's screen time is largely parent-controlled. The eight-year-old has started to have opinions, access, and in some houses, devices of their own. The sleep-disrupting effects of blue light that we covered in Chapter 2 are landing on a brain that is simultaneously more susceptible to stimulation and more capable of hiding it.

The school-age child who was on a tablet for two hours after dinner is not going to announce "I am too stimulated to sleep." They are going to lie in bed, unable to sleep, increasingly frustrated, and tell you "I'm not tired" — which is true, because you accidentally made it true.

What this age needs

- **A hard screen cutoff, not a soft one.** Not "try to finish up soon." A specific time, a specific device handoff, no exceptions. We'll talk about how to install this without World War Three in Chapter 6.

- **A wind-down activity that isn't a screen.** Reading is the gold standard. Not because it's virtuous but because it's genuinely soporific — a good book in a quiet room with a dim light is one of the most reliable sleep-onset tools that exists, and it doesn't require you to do anything once the book is in their hands.
- **Closing the negotiation window.** This age has figured out that bedtime is a conversation. Your job is to make it a non-conversation — not through harshness, but through consistency so total and boring that there is simply nothing to negotiate. We'll cover exactly how in Chapter 5.
- **A bedtime that accounts for their actual school schedule.** An eight-year-old who needs to be up at 6:45am needs to be asleep by 9pm at the latest for the nine to eleven hours of sleep this age range requires. Work backwards from wake time. Most parents work forwards from whenever dinner ended, which is how you end up with a ten-year-old getting seven hours of sleep and wondering why their teacher says they seem distracted.

Bucket Three: The Tween and Early Teen (Ages 11–13)

What it looks like

You were in a deep sleep.

Maybe tonight was the night — the high sleep score on the Garmin sleep tracker device, the unbroken eight hours, the morning where you wake up feeling like an actual human being instead of a software update running on failing hardware.

This was George on this night. Then...

What is that noise?

Who is in the house?

Why are dishes rattling?

George, from his bed, doing the threat assessment that parents do at 1:30am — running through the list of possible explanations, most of which are benign, one of which is a burglar who has inexplicably decided to make himself something to eat.

Footsteps on the stairs.

George looks at the stairs.

It's Patrick.

"Patrick!!! It's 1:30 in the morning!!! You have school tomorrow!!! What are you doing?!"

Patrick, apparently untroubled by the temperature of this reception, "I couldn't sleep."

You look at him. He looks fine. He looks, in fact, *awake* — genuinely, comfortably awake, in the way that you will not be again until approximately 9am.

And he is proudly smiling.

"Did you— are you eating something?"

"I made a cheeseburger."

A pause.

"And a milkshake."

George asks, "Who made that?!

Patrick smiles and says proudly, "I did"

"When did you learn to cook?!" George says.

George stared at his son for a moment. The cheeseburger smelled genuinely good. It had been a long night.

"...Can I have a bite?"

George continues to stare at him. He stares back. Somewhere in this moment is a question we don't even know how to begin asking, which is: *how did we get here, what are the rules, and does he have a math test today?*

He does. He does have a math test today.

Then, returning to the matter at hand. George says, *"You are never going to wake up in the morning. I will definitely be pouring water on your head."*

Patrick considered this. *"I like that,"* he said.

He was not being difficult. He meant it. Trickling water on Patrick's head has since become a legitimate, semi-official wake-up strategy in our house on the mornings when nothing else reaches him. We have made peace with this. You do what works.

What's actually happening

We covered the biology of this in Chapter 2, but let's put it plainly here in the context of what you're actually dealing with:

Your tween or early teen is not staying up late to upset you. They are not staying up late because they have no self-discipline. They are staying up late because their circadian rhythm has physically shifted, their melatonin doesn't rise until late in the evening, and their brain is — right now, tonight, at midnight — doing some of its most active development work. The adolescent brain undergoes more reconstruction between the ages of eleven and fourteen than at any point since infancy. A lot of that work happens during sleep, and a lot of it happens *later* in the sleep cycle than in younger children.

This is also the age where the **phone becomes the central variable.** Not the family iPad. Not the TV in the living room. Their phone. In their room. Under the pillow. Buzzing with the social world that this age group is, neurologically, more dependent on than any other. The tween brain is wired — again, not metaphorically, *actually wired* — to prioritize peer connection above almost everything else. The phone at midnight is not just a screen. It is a social lifeline that their brain is telling them, urgently, is more important than sleep.

You are not competing with a bad habit. You are competing with dopamine, melatonin suppression, social anxiety, FOMO, and a device engineered by some of the smartest behavioral psychologists on the planet to be impossible to put down.

This is why "just take the phone" — while sometimes necessary — is not a complete strategy. We need to replace what the phone is giving them with something else. That's a longer conversation, and we have it in Chapter 6.

What this age needs

- **A realistic bedtime, not an aspirational one.** A thirteen-year-old who is being told to be asleep by 9:30pm when their melatonin doesn't rise until 11 is being set up to lie in bed awake for ninety minutes resenting you. A more realistic target for this age — especially on school nights — is 10 to 10:30pm, with a genuine wind-down starting at 9:30.

- **The phone out of the room.** Not silenced. Not face-down. *Out of the room.* This is the single highest-leverage intervention for teen sleep, and it is also the one most likely to cause a diplomatic incident. We'll give you the script for that conversation in Chapter 6.
- **Some autonomy inside the structure.** The tween who had zero input into their bedtime routine will resist it. The tween who helped design it — who chose the wind-down activity, who negotiated the light-out time within a reasonable range — has buy-in. Not full control. Buy-in. There's a difference, and it matters enormously at this age.

- **Understanding over enforcement.** This is the age where *explaining the why* starts to actually work. Patrick, told that his math test performance is directly correlated to sleep quality in a way he can see on his own Garmin data, is more persuadable than Patrick who is just told to go to bed. If he has a sleep tracker. Use it. Make it his data, his experiment, his result. Thirteen-year-olds respond to evidence about their own performance in a way they never respond to your authority.

The One Table You Actually Need

Age	Sleep Needed	Realistic Bedtime	Biggest Saboteur	Key Strategy
2-5	11-13 Hours	7:00-7:30pm	Missed window / separation anxiety	Consistent sequence, bridge object
6-10	9-11 Hours	8:00-8:30pm	Screens, negotiation, opportunity cost	Hard screen cutoff, wind-down reading
11-13	8-10 Hours	10:00-10:30pm	Phone, circadian shift	Phone out of room, autonomy + data

Save this table. Screenshot it.
It will answer approximately half the questions you currently have.

Now that we know who we're dealing with — and why each version of them is a distinct challenge — we can actually build the thing that solves it.

The routine.

Not a theoretical routine. Not the routine from a book that was written for someone else's child. A real, flexible, actually-buildable routine that works in a house where people are tired and time is short and the Lego is always on the floor and Patrick is always hungry.

That's Chapter 4.

Chapter 4: The Routine That Actually Sticks — And Why Yours Didn't →

Chapter 4:

The Routine That Actually Sticks — And Why Yours Didn't

Here is the most common bedtime routine in America:

Someone looks up from whatever they're doing, realizes it's later than they thought, and says "okay, bedtime" with the energy of a person who has already lost.

The kids protest. There is negotiation. Someone needs a snack. Someone needs to find their stuffed animal. Someone needs to tell you something important that absolutely cannot wait until morning. The process takes forty-five minutes and ends with you sitting on the edge of a bed in the dark, slightly resentful, waiting for the breathing to slow so you can escape.

You do this again tomorrow night.

On one particular night, George gave up entirely and went to bed before the kids.

Julene was in charge. George was done — unilaterally, finally, without negotiation. He said goodnight and went upstairs.

And then it happened.

He was awakened by chasing. By giggling. By the specific laughter of children who know they're supposed to be in bed and have decided this makes it funnier. And underneath all of it, Julene's voice — escalating — *"Get to bed! GET. TO. BED!"*

This was our house on that night.

This is not a routine. This is a recurring crisis with a bedtime theme. And the reason we know so much about fixing it is that we spent a long time living inside it.

A real routine is different in one fundamental way: **it runs on autopilot.** Not yours — your kid's. The goal of a bedtime routine is to wire a sequence of events so deeply into your child's brain that their body begins the shutdown process automatically when the sequence starts — before you've said a word, before there's anything to resist, before the negotiation window even opens.

This takes about two weeks to build. It takes about two nights to destroy. So consistency is the whole game. Not perfection — consistency. There is a difference, and we'll come back to it.

Here are three routines. Find your bucket. Build your version. Start Thursday if tonight is already a write-off.

Routine One: The Little Ones (Ages 2–5)

The goal

You are not trying to get your toddler to want to go to sleep. You are trying to make bedtime so predictable, so safe, and so identical every night that their brain stops treating it as an event worth resisting and starts treating it as just the thing that happens next.

The window

This age group has a sleep window that is earlier than most parents expect and less forgiving than most parents would like. For most children between two and five, optimal sleep onset is **between 7:00 and 7:30pm.** Not 8. Not 8:30. The parents who swear their toddler "just isn't tired until nine" have, in most cases, accidentally trained a second wind by consistently missing the window until the body adapted.

Start the routine **forty-five minutes before your target sleep time.** If you want them asleep by 7:30, the routine starts at 6:45. Put it in your phone as a recurring alarm. Call it whatever you want. Call it "The Gauntlet." Just make it non-negotiable.

The sequence

Step 1: The Warning (5 minutes before routine starts) Before you do anything else, give a transition warning. "In five minutes we're starting bedtime." This sounds small. It is not small. Toddlers and preschoolers have almost no control over their lives, and abrupt transitions — being pulled out of play without warning — spike the stress response immediately. The warning doesn't give them control. It gives them *preparation.* That's enough to reduce the initial resistance significantly.

Step 2: Bath or Wash-Up (10–15 minutes) A warm bath is genuinely sleep-promoting — body temperature drops after you get out of warm water, and that temperature drop is one of the physical triggers for sleep onset. If a full bath every night isn't realistic, a quick warm washcloth on the face and hands works. The point is the warm-to-cool transition and the sensory signal that the day is ending.

Step 3: Pajamas and Teeth (5 minutes) Make this the same every night. Same order. Pajamas first, then teeth, or teeth first then pajamas — pick one and never deviate. The sameness is the point. Their brain is now three steps into a sequence it recognizes. The shutdown is beginning whether they know it or not.

Step 4: The One Book (10–15 minutes) One book. Not three. Not "one more." The same book they've requested for the last six weeks, which you can now recite in your sleep, which is fine because that means it's working exactly as intended. A familiar book requires less cognitive engagement than a new one — for them and for you — which means the brain is already idling down. Read it the same way every time. Same voices. Same pace. Boring is a feature, not a bug.

Step 5: The Closing Ritual (3–5 minutes) This is the anchor. A short, identical sequence of words or actions that signals: *this is the end.* It can be a song — the same song, always. A specific series of hugs and kisses in a specific order that has a name your kid gave it. A quiet prayer if that's part of your family. Three things they're grateful for. Whatever it is, make it short, make it sweet, and make it *exactly the same every night.* This is the moment the brain files away as "sleep is coming now." Over time, the closing ritual alone will start producing drowsiness. You are conditioning sleep. Pavlov had a bell. You have a song about stars.

Step 6: The Pre-Empt (1 minute) Before you turn out the light, do this: *"I'm going to check on you in five minutes. Your water is right here. Your [stuffed animal] is right here. Is there anything you need before I turn the light off?"*

You are closing the loopholes before they find them. The water request, the forgotten item, the "I need to tell you something" — you are preempting all of it with one question. Answer whatever comes up. Then turn off the light with the calm finality of someone who has genuinely handled everything and is not available for follow-up questions.

Step 7: The Check-In (5 minutes later) Go back. Poke your head in. Say something quiet and boring. "Just checking in. Everything good? Okay. Goodnight." Then leave.

This is the move that cuts the callback loop in half. The child who knows you're coming back doesn't need to call for you. The uncertainty — *will they come back?* — is what drives the repeated requests. Remove the uncertainty. Make the check-in part of the routine. After a week or two, you can start extending the time before the check-in. Eventually it becomes unnecessary because the trust is established.

When it falls apart

It will fall apart. Plan for two things:

Overtiredness: If you missed the window and your toddler is past tired and into manic, compress the routine. Skip the long bath. Do a quick wash. Do the book. Do the closing ritual. Get them horizontal as fast as possible. A full routine on an overtired toddler is a forty-five minute disaster. A short one is a twenty-minute one. Pick your battle size.

The regression: Every toddler will, at some point, go through a week or two where the routine that was working suddenly stops working. This is normal. It is not a sign that the routine is broken. It is a sign that they are going through something — a developmental leap, a disruption at daycare, a new sibling, a weird phase — and the routine needs to hold steady while they get through it. Do not abandon the routine during a regression. The routine is the life raft. Hold onto it.

Routine Two: The School-Age Kid (Ages 6–10)

The goal

You are trying to do two things at once: create a sequence the body recognizes as the lead-up to sleep, and close the negotiation window before it opens. At this age, consistency still drives the biology, but you now also have a child who is watching for gaps in your commitment and will find them faster than you expect.

The window

Work backwards from wake time. Take the hour your child needs to be up. Subtract ten hours. That's your target sleep time. An eight-year-old up at 6:45am needs to be asleep by 8:45pm. Not in bed. *Asleep.* Which means in bed by 8:15, lights out by 8:30, falling asleep by 8:45 if things go well.

The routine starts **one hour before lights-out.** Set the alarm. Honor it.

The sequence

Step 1: The Screen Cutoff (60 minutes before lights-out) This is the non-negotiable that makes everything else possible. One hour before lights-out, all screens off. Not "finishing this episode." Not "five more minutes." Off. The device goes somewhere that is not their room — the kitchen counter, the charging station in the hallway, wherever you've designated.

The reason for one hour is melatonin math: blue light suppresses melatonin release, and the suppression doesn't end the moment the screen goes off. It takes time — up to an hour — for the melatonin system to recover and begin rising normally. A screen cutoff at thirty minutes before bed is better than nothing. Sixty minutes is where you actually get the benefit.

Expect resistance to this for the first week. Hold the line. By week two it's just the rule.

Step 2: The Wind-Down Activity (20–30 minutes) This is the replacement for the screen, and it matters that it be something genuinely absorbing. The goal is to give their brain something to do that is low-stimulation but not boring enough to invite negotiation. Reading is ideal. Drawing works. Lego with calm music works, though it risks the "I just need to finish this one part" problem — set a specific stopping point before they start. A puzzle. A journal. Anything that is quiet, screenless, and can be done independently in their room.

Do not require them to be in bed for this. Let them be in bed, on the floor, wherever. The activity is the transition. The location is secondary.

Step 3: Hygiene (10 minutes) Teeth. Face. Whatever your household standard is. Same order, every night. By this age they can do most of this independently, which is good — the autonomy makes them less likely to resist it. Your job is to verify, not supervise.

Step 4: The Check-In Conversation (5–10 minutes) This is the move that most bedtime routines skip, and it's one of the highest-value things you can do for a school-age child. Before lights-out, sit on the edge of the bed — or stand in the doorway if you're in a compressed-timeline night — and ask one open question. Not "how was your day" (useless, generates "fine"). Something specific: *"What was the most annoying thing that happened today?"* or *"Did anything weird happen at school?"* or *"What are you thinking about right now?"*

This serves two purposes. First, it gives the child a chance to off-load whatever is running in the background — the social worry, the thing that happened at lunch, the test they're anxious about — so it's not rattling around keeping them awake. Second, it is the connection moment that this age still needs, even though they're increasingly good at pretending they don't. The child who has had five minutes of genuine parental attention at bedtime separates more easily than the child who hasn't.

Keep it short. Five to ten minutes. This is not the time for a long conversation. If something significant comes up, acknowledge it and tell them you'll talk more tomorrow. Then follow up tomorrow. The bedtime conversation is a release valve, not a therapy session.

One night at check-in, Juney decided it was a good time to talk about how sad she had been at school that day.

An hour later she was smiling. Happy. Unburdened. Fully processed.

And hungry for a bedtime snack.

Was it a perfect bedtime? No. Was it time we would trade back? Also no. The check-in is not always efficient. Sometimes it is the most important ten minutes of your child's day, disguised as a delay tactic. You don't always know which one you're in until you're already an hour into it.

Show up anyway.

Step 5: The Close (3–5 minutes) Lights off, or nightlight on — whatever your kid prefers. A brief, warm closing. You don't need a ritual as elaborate as the toddler version, but some version of a consistent sign-off still works. "Goodnight, I love you, see you in the morning" said the same way every night is enough. The sameness signals finality.

Then leave. With the energy of someone who is done for the evening. Not tentative. Not bracing for a callback. Done.

Step 6: The Boundary Hold Here is where this age diverges from the toddler routine. When the callback comes — and it will come — you have one job: be boring. Don't engage with the content of the request. Don't problem-solve. Don't negotiate. Appear in the doorway, say something low-energy and final — *"Everything's fine. Go to sleep. I love you. Goodnight."* — and leave.

The callbacks will escalate for a few nights before they stop. This is normal. They are testing whether the new normal is actually the new normal. Every time you hold the boring, loving, completely final close, you are one night closer to a child who stops testing it because they know the answer.

When it falls apart

The homework ambush: The nine-year-old who announces at 8pm that there is a project due tomorrow that you are only now hearing about. This will happen. Have a rule established in advance: homework is done before the wind-down activity starts. If it isn't, the wind-down is shorter. If it *really* isn't — if there is a legitimate crisis — handle the homework and compress everything else. Do not skip the closing ritual entirely. Even a five-minute abbreviated version of the routine is better than no routine, because the brain needs some version of the signal.

The sleepover disruption: One late night with a friend can push the internal clock later and make the following bedtime harder. Don't try to force an early bedtime the night after a sleepover. Split the difference — aim for thirty minutes earlier than the sleepover time — and get back to normal the night after that.

Routine Three: The Tween and Early Teen (Ages 11–13)

The goal

You are not trying to tuck them in. You are trying to create conditions — biological, environmental, and social — that make sleep possible for a brain that is actively working against you on the timing front. The goal at this age is a sustainable system they have some ownership over, because a system they resent will be dismantled the first chance they get.

The window

A thirteen-year-old with a circadian shift of one to two hours needs a realistic target, not an aspirational one. For most tweens and early teens on a school night, **lights-out between 10:00 and 10:30pm** is achievable and will produce enough sleep if the morning alarm isn't brutal. If your school start time requires a 6:15am wake-up, you are dealing with a structural problem — school start times and adolescent sleep biology are genuinely misaligned, and that is not your fault or your kid's — but a 10:00 lights-out is still better than 11:30.

The routine starts **ninety minutes before lights-out.** If lights-out is 10pm, the routine starts at 8:30.

The sequence

Step 1: The Phone Handoff (90 minutes before lights-out) This is the hard one. This is the one they'll argue about most. This is also the one that matters most.

The phone does not sleep in their room. Full stop. Not face-down, not silenced, not in airplane mode. In another room. Charging. Unavailable.

Here is how you make this conversation survivable: you do not frame it as punishment or distrust. You frame it as biology. *"Your phone is producing light that is chemically blocking your melatonin. This isn't me deciding you can't be trusted. This is me not letting a device sabotage your sleep. We can look at your Garmin data together if you want proof."*

You offer an alternative. A dedicated alarm clock so they don't need the phone for that. A physical book, a journal, a sketchbook — something that fills the social/entertainment function without the blue light and the infinite scroll. You acknowledge that this is annoying. You hold the line anyway.

Expect a diplomatic incident the first week. Hold the line.

Step 2: The Wind-Down Block (60–45 minutes before lights-out) This age can largely self-manage the wind-down if you've set up the conditions correctly. The phone is gone. The environment is low-stimulation. What they do in this block is somewhat up to them — reading, drawing, a journal, low-key music, even a calm podcast — as long as it is screenless and horizontal-adjacent.

Giving them ownership of this block is strategic. The tween who chose their own wind-down activity is infinitely more likely to actually do it than the tween who was told what to do. Let them pick. Veto screens. Otherwise, step back.

Step 3: Hygiene (15 minutes before lights-out) By this age this is entirely their responsibility. Your job is to have the expectation, not to supervise it. A brief, non-nagging check — "did you do teeth?" asked once, in passing — is sufficient. Pick your battles. Teeth matter. The order in which they do everything does not.

Step 4: The Optional Check-In (10 minutes before lights-out) This one is optional in the sense that you cannot force a thirteen-year-old to have a conversation with you. But it is not optional in the sense that it matters enormously and you should keep showing up for it even when it goes nowhere.

Knock. Poke your head in. Ask something low-stakes. "You good?" is fine. "How'd the math thing go?" if there was a math thing. The goal is not a deep conversation — though sometimes you'll get one, and those are gifts. The goal is the signal: *I'm here, I'm interested, the door is open.*

Some nights they'll grunt. Some nights they'll tell you something that makes you glad you asked. Keep showing up. The tween who knows the check-in is coming — who knows you'll be there regardless of whether they want to talk — carries less to bed with them than the one who doesn't.

Step 5: The Close This age doesn't want a ritual. They want you to say goodnight and leave without making it weird. So say goodnight and leave without making it weird. "Goodnight, love you" said without hovering, without the lingering, without the checking-whether-the-phone-is-really-gone energy.

Check the phone thing before the close. Once. Calmly. Then close with warmth and leave with confidence.

Step 6: The Garmin Strategy This is specific to Patrick but applicable to any tween who has a fitness tracker or sleep tracker, and increasingly many of them do.

Stop telling Patrick to go to sleep. Start showing Patrick his data.

Pull up his sleep scores from the weeks when he went to bed by 10 versus the weeks when he was up until 1am. Show him his REM numbers. Show him his math test performance — which, if you've been paying attention, correlates pretty neatly with whether he slept. Don't lecture. Just show him the data and ask him what he thinks.

Thirteen-year-olds are deeply interested in their own performance. They are profoundly uninterested in doing what you say. These two facts can be turned into an advantage. Make sleep his project, not your rule. Make the Garmin score his metric, not your concern. Step back and let him connect his own dots.

It won't work overnight. It will work over time. And it will work far better, and last far longer, than any version of "because I said so" ever will.

The One Rule That Applies to All Three

Whatever routine you build, the rule is this: **do it the same way for fourteen consecutive nights before you decide whether it's working.**

Not two nights. Not five. Fourteen.

When we decided to actually commit to fourteen nights — a real decision, made out loud, to each other — there was a problem.

One of us knew the other wasn't going to make it the distance.

The problem was that it was both of us. We both knew it about ourselves and suspected it about each other, and neither of us said it, because sometimes you decide to believe the better version of the story and see what happens.

We'll tell you what happened in Chapter 7. For now: fourteen nights. Commit to it before you need to believe it.

Behavioral change in children — and in adults — requires repetition past the point of initial resistance. The first few nights of any new routine, the child is testing whether it's real. Nights five through ten, they're starting to accept it but still looking for cracks. By night fourteen, the brain has begun to encode the sequence as habit and the body has begun to respond to the cues.

Most parents abandon a routine at night three because the resistance is high and it doesn't seem to be working. Night three is the worst night. Night three is also one night before it starts to get easier. Don't quit on night three.

You now have the routine. What you don't yet have is a strategy for the forces that will try to derail it — the late homework, the screen negotiation, the meltdown, the night where everything falls apart and you make every mistake and the whole thing starts over.

That's what Chapter 5 is for.

Chapter 5: The Ways We Make It Worse — A Loving Self-Audit →

Chapter 5:

The Ways We Make It Worse — A Loving Self-Audit

This chapter is not here to make you feel bad.

It is here to make you feel *seen.* And also slightly caught. And then, hopefully, understood — because every single thing in this chapter has been done by good, loving, intelligent parents who were tired and improvising and just trying to get to the other side of the evening.

Including, it must be said, the authors of this book.

We'll get to that.

The bedtime strategies in Chapter 4 will work. They will work reliably, in real houses, for real children, if you do them consistently. But there are a handful of things — common, understandable, extremely human things — that will quietly dismantle every good system you build if you don't recognize them for what they are.

This is the loving self-audit. Read it without judgment. Nod at the ones that apply. Try not to do them again starting tonight.

The Negotiation Trap

Here is how it starts.

You say "bedtime."

Your child says "five more minutes."

You think: *five minutes is nothing. Five minutes is fine. I can hold out for five minutes and then we're done.*

You say "fine. Five minutes."

Your child has just learned something important: *bedtime is a number you can move.*

This is the negotiation trap, and it is almost impossible to avoid falling into at least occasionally, because the offer of five minutes sounds so reasonable. It's not a big ask. You're not giving up much. And the path of least resistance right now is to say yes and deal with the next thing in five minutes.

But here's what's actually happening: you are not agreeing to five more minutes. You are agreeing to a *system* — a system in which bedtime is understood by your child to be an opening position rather than a final one. And once that system is in place, every future bedtime begins with a negotiation, because why wouldn't it? It worked last time. And the time before. And basically every time.

The negotiation trap is especially insidious because the amounts stay small. Nobody negotiates for two extra hours. They negotiate for five minutes. Ten minutes. "Just until this episode is over." "Just until I finish this chapter." The individual asks are so modest that each one seems easy to grant. It's only when you add them up — when you look at the clock and realize you've been "five more minutes"-ing for forty-five minutes — that you see the hole you've been digging.

The fix: Bedtime is not a negotiation. It is an announcement. The routine exists specifically so there is no opening offer — the sequence is already in motion before anyone has a chance to open a discussion. And on the nights when the negotiation attempt comes anyway, the answer is warm, boring, and final: *"Nope. Bedtime. Let's go."* No debate. No engagement with the logic of the request. The energy of someone who genuinely has nothing further to discuss.

The Bribe Escalation

Let us tell you about the ice cream.

It was a night — not unlike many nights in our house — where bedtime had already gone sideways. Our daughter, Juney, had been asked to stay in bed. She had agreed to stay in bed. She had then gotten out of bed. She had been returned to bed. She had gotten out again. We were tired. She was allegedly tired but showing no evidence of it. The will to hold the line was evaporating.

And then someone — and we will not assign blame here, but it was not George — had an idea.

"What if she gets ice cream tomorrow if she stays in bed tonight?"

Reader, we gave her the ice cream that night. In bed. Before she'd even stayed in it.

She got out of bed three more times.

The ice cream bribe is not a parenting failure. It is a completely rational response to an irrational situation made by two adults who had been awake since 5am and had simply run out of better options. We have been there. You have been there. Everyone has been there.

But here is what the ice cream actually taught our daughter: *if I hold out long enough, something good happens.* Not "if I go to bed nicely, bedtime is peaceful." If I resist, escalate, and make the situation uncomfortable enough — eventually a reward appears.

This is, from a behavioral psychology standpoint, almost the worst possible signal you can send. You have just rewarded the exact behavior you were trying to extinguish. Tomorrow night, she will start the resistance earlier, because she has data.

Bribes work in the moment. They reliably make the next moment worse. The only exception is bribes that are built *into* the routine as a consistent, earned reward — a sticker chart for the younger ones, a small privilege earned by a week of smooth bedtimes — because these reward the *pattern* rather than the *resistance.* That's a different thing. We'll talk about it in Chapter 7.

The ice cream in bed, though? We retired that one. Eventually.

The Re-Tuck

After the ice cream, our daughter got out of bed.

She did not get out of bed asking for ice cream. She got out of bed asking Julene to come tuck her in.

Again.

Julene went.

Our daughter got out of bed again. Asked again. Julene went again.

This happened four times.

Now. Here is the thing about the re-tuck, and we want to say this with genuine tenderness because it comes from a good place: **the re-tuck is not for the child.** Or rather, it is not *only* for the child. It is also for the parent who cannot bear to hear their child ask for them and not respond. Who feels, somewhere underneath the exhaustion, that every tuck is a moment of connection and what kind of parent refuses that?

A reasonable parent, as it turns out. One who understands that the re-tuck — like the ice cream, like the five more minutes — is teaching a lesson the opposite of the one you intend. The lesson is: *if I ask for Mom, Mom comes.* Which is a beautiful lesson in unconditional love and a catastrophic lesson in bedtime boundaries.

The re-tuck also has a quality that makes it particularly hard to break: it is physically, emotionally comforting to do. You go in. The room is quiet. Your child is small and warm and smells like soap. They look at you like you are the best person in the world. You tuck the blanket. You kiss the forehead. You feel, for one moment, like a genuinely good parent.

Then you do it again thirty minutes later and it is less magical.

The fix is the pre-empt from Chapter 4 — the closing sequence that anticipates the need and meets it before it generates a request. The child who has been thoroughly tucked, given a bridge object, given a check-in time, and told everything is handled has less to ask for. Not zero. But less. And on the nights where the request still comes — *"can you tuck me in again?"* — the answer is a one-time, warm, final repeat of the close. Once. Not four times. Once. "I already tucked you in. Everything's fine. I love you. Goodnight."

Julene gets full credit for figuring this out. Not because George didn't understand the theory — he did — but because Julene was the one who actually held the line on the night it mattered, which is a different thing entirely from understanding a theory.

She went in once. She did the close. She left.

Juney called for her again. Julene stood in the hallway for a moment — aware of exactly what was happening, aware of exactly how easy it would be to go back in — and did not go back in.

There was crying. There was the specific sound of a child who cannot believe this is happening.

Then there was quiet.

George would like the record to reflect that he was very supportive of this from the other room.

The Screen Compromise That Isn't

This one requires a confession that is almost too embarrassing to include, except that it is so universal that leaving it out would be doing you a disservice.

Our daughter, on more than one occasion, has deployed the following negotiation: *"Can I watch my iPad for just ten minutes? I promise I'll stay in bed if you let me do that."*

This offer sounds reasonable. Ten minutes. She stays in bed. You get to stop managing the situation. It is a clean deal.

We took the deal.

We then fell asleep — exhausted adults falling asleep at the hour that exhausted adults fall asleep — and were awakened later by the sound of Patrick making himself a cheeseburger at 1:30am, and in the process of that whole investigation discovered that our daughter was *still watching her iPad.*

Two hours later.

In the dark.

Alone.

She had not moved. She had not needed anything. She had simply continued watching, in the quiet and the dark, with the focus and commitment of a person who has found something good and intends to see it through.

The ten-minute screen compromise fails for two reasons.

First: there is no enforcement mechanism. Once you've fallen asleep — and you will fall asleep, because you are a human being who is tired — the ten minutes becomes whatever she decides it is. She is not being defiant. She is just watching her show. The deal she made with you has dissolved the moment you stopped being conscious.

Second: the ten minutes of screen before bed undoes the wind-down you spent the previous hour building. Even if it *were* ten minutes — even in the version of events where she actually stops — the blue light exposure and the stimulation of whatever she's watching spikes her system right at the moment it most needs to be quiet. You have just spent an hour getting her ready to sleep and then handed her something that chemically prevents it.

The screen deal is not a compromise. It is a surrender that takes two hours to fully reveal itself.

The fix is a hard screen cutoff with no negotiation and no exceptions. We covered the biology in Chapter 2. The emotional logic of the fix is this: you are not taking the screen because you're mean. You are taking the screen because you know what it does to her brain and you love her enough to be unpopular about it. That framing helps on the nights when holding the line feels unkind. It does not make the child less annoyed. It makes you clearer on why you're doing it.

The Phone-In-Pocket Problem

We would be leaving out a significant piece of the picture if we didn't include this one.

You have told your child to put away their device. You are delivering this instruction with appropriate parental authority.

And then George disappears into the bathroom for a very long time.

A very. Very. Very. Long. Time.

Julene walked in.

He was on his phone. Scrolling. Smiling.

Not a work emergency. Not something urgent. Just a man who had found a quiet room and was enjoying it, on a device, at the exact moment the household rule about devices was being enforced on everyone else.

Children notice everything. They noticed this too. We know because they mentioned it.

The fix is simple and hard at the same time: during the bedtime sequence, the phone stays in the kitchen. Not because you don't need it. Because the twenty minutes you spend on the actual bedtime routine is more important than whatever is happening on the phone, and because your kid is watching, and because what they learn from watching you is more durable than anything you say.

The Inconsistency Tax

Here is the most expensive mistake on this list.

You did the routine perfectly on Monday. On Tuesday it went reasonably well. On Wednesday there was a thing — a work thing, an exhaustion thing, a night when everyone was running late and the homework was a crisis and dinner happened at 8pm — and the routine didn't happen. On Thursday you tried to reinstate it and your child looked at you like you'd suggested something brand new.

"We don't have to do all that. We didn't do it yesterday."

This is the inconsistency tax. Every night you skip the routine, you pay for it on the next two or three nights. The child's brain, which was beginning to encode the sequence as normal, resets its uncertainty. The testing behavior comes back. The callbacks return. You are not starting from zero, exactly — but you are starting from further back than you were on Tuesday.

This is the reason "consistency" appears in every chapter of this book, in slightly different language, with slightly different emphasis. It is not a platitude. It is the actual mechanism. The routine works because repetition builds neural encoding. Gaps in the repetition interrupt the encoding. The brain needs the same signal, in the same sequence, on the same schedule, for long enough that it stops treating the signal as information and starts treating it as weather — something that just happens, reliably, without requiring a response.

You will miss nights. Life is not a controlled experiment. But understand the tax you're paying when you do, and get back on the routine the next night without drama. Don't announce the return. Don't apologize for the gap. Just do the thing. The brain will pick up where it left off faster than you expect.

The Self-Audit Checklist

Before we move to Chapter 6, here's a quick honest list. Read it privately. Answer it privately. No judgment.

In the last two weeks, have you:

- Agreed to "just five more minutes" more than twice? ✓
- Offered a reward in the middle of a bedtime standoff? ✓
- Gone back in for a re-tuck more than once in a single night? ✓
- Let a screen happen in the last hour before bed because you needed the peace? ✓
- Checked your own phone while telling your child to put theirs away? ✓

- Skipped the routine entirely because the night was already a write-off? ✓
- Made a threat at bedtime that you didn't follow through on? ✓

If you checked three or more of those, you are a completely normal parent who has been doing their best under conditions that are not designed to make this easy. Nothing on that list makes you a bad parent. Everything on that list, done consistently, makes bedtime harder than it needs to be.

Now you know. That's the whole point of the audit.

Chapter 6 is where we go after the external forces — the screens, the fears, the hunger, the 9:45pm water phenomenon, and the specific, infuriating phrase *"but I'm not even tired"* — with specific fixes for each one.

Chapter 7 is the three-night reset. The thing you do starting tonight.

We're almost at the actionable part. Hang in there.

Chapter 6: The Saboteurs — Screens, Fears, Hunger, and the 9pm "I Need Water" Phenomenon →

Chapter 6:

The Saboteurs — Screens, Fears, Hunger, and the 9pm "I Need Water" Phenomenon

---

You did everything right.

The routine happened. The sequence was followed. The close was warm and final and you left the room with genuine confidence. You poured yourself something. You sat down. You exhaled.

And then.

"Can you leave the lights on?"

The saboteurs are the forces that operate outside the routine — the fears, the hunger, the thirst, the very specific anxieties that seem to activate exclusively between 8pm and midnight, and the devices that have developed, over time, a near-perfect ability to find the gaps in your defenses.

They are not random. They follow patterns. And once you know the patterns, you can build around them instead of being ambushed by them every single night.

Saboteur One: The Fear

It starts reasonably enough.

"Can you leave the lights on?"

Fine. The nightlight is on. The hallway light is on. This is manageable.

"Can you open my closet door and keep those lights on too?"

You open the closet. You leave the lights on. You say goodnight again. You go back to whatever you were doing.

Twenty minutes pass.

Ruffle-ruffle.

Tiny steps in the hallway. The specific sound of small feet that are trying to be quiet and aren't quite managing it. Your door opens.

"Mommy, can I sleep with you? I'm scared."

And here is where it happens — the moment that undoes everything, the move that is so instinctively, obviously correct that it almost cannot be resisted.

Julene says yes. Of course she says yes.

George will admit here — once, and only once, *a-hem* — that on at least one of these nights, he was pretending to be asleep. He knew exactly what would be required of him if he were awake. He knew what the right move was. He simply did not have the energy for it, and he made a calculated decision to be unconscious.

He knew Julene would say yes.

Julene, reading this paragraph for the first time, laughed out loud.

"It has been far more than one time. You think I don't know?"

She knew. She has always known. The stillness was not convincing. The breathing was not convincing. A woman who has shared a bed with someone for years knows the difference between asleep and aggressively pretending.

George was not as invisible as he thought.

He was also, on those nights, not wrong that she would say yes. That's the part we both had to fix.

What's actually happening

Fear at bedtime is real. We want to say that plainly before anything else. The child who says they're scared is not, in most cases, performing. The dark is genuinely threatening to a young brain that has not yet fully developed the capacity to distinguish between *feels dangerous* and *is dangerous.* Monsters are not real. The fear of monsters is.

What is also true is that fear, like every other bedtime behavior, responds to the conditions you create around it. A child whose fear is consistently met with immediate parental presence in the bed will, over time, require parental presence in the bed to feel safe. The solution becomes the problem. The comfort that was meant to be temporary becomes structural.

This is not because your child is manipulative. It is because you have — accidentally, lovingly, completely understandably — trained a system. The system is: *I feel scared, I go to Mom and Dad's room, the fear goes away.* From the child's perspective this is a perfect system. From yours it is a system that will be in operation until someone changes it.

The other thing happening: **fear is also sometimes not fear.** The child who has been on a screen for two hours before bed, whose cortisol is elevated from the bedtime argument, whose melatonin has been suppressed by blue light, who is lying in the dark with a revved-up nervous system and nothing to do — that child will find something to be scared of. The fear is real, but the root cause is stimulation and dysregulation, not darkness. Fix the routine and the fear often diminishes on its own.

The fix

For the lights: Give them control within limits. A nightlight — their choice of nightlight, ideally, something they picked — stays on. The closet lights do not. The hallway light can stay on at low level. The principle is: we address the real concern with a real solution, and we don't keep escalating the lighting conditions until the room looks like a dental office.

For the fear itself: The goal is to build felt safety *inside their room* rather than relocating them to yours. This means:

A consistent closing ritual that ends with reassurance — not effusive, not lengthy, just calm and certain. *"You're safe. I'm right down the hall. The nightlight is on. I'll check on you."* Said the same way every night. Said with the energy of someone who genuinely believes it, because you do.

The check-in, which we covered in Chapter 4, does double duty here. A child who knows you're coming back in five minutes has a concrete anchor for the waiting. The fear lives in the uncertainty — *what if something happens while they're gone?* The check-in answers that question before it becomes a crisis.

For the "can I sleep with you" request: The answer can be loving and still be no. *"You're safe in your bed. I know it feels scary. Let's go back and I'll sit with you for two minutes."* You return them to their room. You sit — briefly, boringly, not engaging with the drama of the fear. You leave. You do this as many times as necessary, with decreasing enthusiasm each time, until it stops being worth the effort.

Is this harder than just letting them into the bed? Yes. For about a week. After that week, you have a child who can manage the fear in their own room, which is a gift you're giving them that will last years.

The family bed is a real choice that real families make intentionally. That's different. What we're talking about is the 11pm ambush that lands four people in a queen bed because nobody had a plan.

The story request

"Can you tell me a story so I can fall asleep?"

This one deserves its own paragraph because it is so perfectly designed to succeed.

It is, technically, a pro-sleep request. It involves no screens. It requires lying still with eyes closed. It is the exact thing that you, in the abstract, would like your child to be doing. And it requires you to stay in the room, which is the actual goal.

The story request at midnight, from a child who has already been tucked in twice and relocated to your bed and tucked in again, is not a sleep aid. It is a companionship request wearing a sleep aid costume.

The answer is an audiobook. Or a pre-approved podcast for kids. Or a white noise machine with a timer. Something that provides the auditory companionship the child is actually asking for, without requiring your continued physical presence in the room at a time when your presence there is the point.

Set it up before the routine starts. Make it part of the close. *"Your story is ready when you want it."* Hand them the thing. Leave the room. The story plays. You are not in it.

Saboteur Two: The Screen — And the Alarm Clock Defense

Let's talk about the phone.

Specifically, let's talk about the moment you go to remove the phone from your thirteen-year-old's room at 9:30pm and he looks at you with the earnest, slightly injured expression of someone being genuinely wronged and says:

"But Dad, I won't have an alarm clock if you take my phone. That's my alarm."

This is a masterpiece. We want to take a moment to appreciate it before we dismantle it.

It is technically true. His phone is his alarm. You did not provide an alternative. He is not asking to keep the phone for TikTok — he is asking to keep it for a legitimate, responsible, adult-behavior reason. He needs to wake up for school. He is being proactive about this. What kind of parent removes a child's only method of waking up for school?

The argument is airtight. It took him approximately four seconds to construct it. He has probably had it ready for weeks.

You know what is waiting for him on the other side of that alarm clock:

A cheeseburger. A milkshake. Your sleep score, gone.

What's actually happening

Patrick is not wrong that he uses his phone as an alarm. Patrick is also not primarily keeping his phone for the alarm. The alarm is the shield. Behind the shield is the group chat, the YouTube, the social media, the infinite scroll that his brain — for reasons we covered in Chapter 2 — is neurologically primed to find more compelling than sleep at 11pm.

The phone in the room at night is not a neutral object. It is an active participant in the destruction of sleep. It buzzes. It glows. It offers, at any moment of wakeful boredom, an entire social world that is also awake and also on their phones. The teen brain, already shifted later, already resistant to sleep, finds in the phone a perfect companion for the hours when sleep won't come. And then sleep *really* won't come. And then it's 1:30am and someone is making a hot meal.

The research on this is not subtle. Teens who sleep with their phones in their rooms get less sleep, worse sleep, and more disrupted sleep than teens who don't. Not marginally less. Significantly less. An hour or more, on average, per night. Over a school year, that is hundreds of hours of lost sleep accumulated in increments of "just checking one thing."

The fix

The alarm clock argument has a simple answer: buy an alarm clock.

A real one. A cheap one. A dedicated single-purpose device that tells time and makes noise in the morning and does nothing else. Put it on his nightstand. Remove the objection permanently.

This is not optional. If you tell your teenager the phone needs to leave the room and don't provide an alternative for the alarm, you have handed him a valid argument that will be used every night indefinitely. Take the argument away before the conversation happens. Show up with the alarm clock. Set it together. Confirm the time. Hand it to him. Now there's nothing to discuss.

The phone charging station: Establish a place — the kitchen counter, a shelf in the hallway, wherever works in your house — where all family phones charge overnight. Including yours. The rule applies to everyone. This matters enormously: a rule that applies only to the teenager is a rule about power. A rule that applies to the whole family is a rule about values. One of these generates resentment. The other generates, eventually, buy-in.

The explanation, not the decree: As we said in Chapter 3, this age responds to evidence over authority. Have the conversation once, properly — not at bedtime when everyone is tired, but at dinner or in the car, at a neutral moment. Show him the research. Show him his own sleep data if he has a tracker. Make it a conversation, not a ruling.

Then hold the line. The line is: the phone sleeps in the kitchen. Starting tonight. Every night. This is not up for renegotiation.

Expect the first week to be uncomfortable. Hold the line.

By week three, the cheeseburgers will stop.

Saboteur Three: Hunger

There is a version of this that is legitimate and a version of this that is tactical, and they look almost identical.

The legitimate version: your child is actually hungry. Dinner was early, or light, or they didn't eat much because something was wrong with the way the pasta was touching the sauce. Their blood sugar is genuinely low. They need something small and they will sleep better for having had it.

The tactical version: your child is not particularly hungry but has identified hunger as a request you cannot reasonably refuse, because what kind of parent sends their child to bed starving?

The tell is timing and history. A child who is routinely hungry at bedtime has a dinner problem, not a bedtime problem — they need more food earlier, or a small designated pre-bed snack built into the routine so the hunger is anticipated rather than weaponized. A child who is suddenly, urgently hungry only on the nights when the routine is tight and the close was final has discovered an exploit.

The fix: Build a small snack into the routine. For the younger kids, a small snack thirty minutes before the sequence starts — something with protein and fat, not sugar, so it doesn't hit the adenosine system. Cheese, peanut butter, a small bowl of cereal with milk. Nothing exciting. Exciting snacks become the focus of negotiation. Boring snacks close the hunger loophole without opening a new one.

For the older kids and teens — whose actual hunger at 10pm may be genuine, because they are burning enormous amounts of energy growing — a designated, limited, no-drama pre-bed snack option solves this. *"You can have [specific thing] before bed if you're hungry. That's the option. It happens before the phone handoff, not after."*

Structure the snack into the routine so it cannot be used as a delay tactic. Once it's expected, it stops being interesting.

The cheeseburger and milkshake at 1:30am, for the record, is a separate category of problem. That is not hunger deploying tactics. That is a teenager with a shifted circadian rhythm, a functional kitchen, and more culinary ambition than you expected at that hour. We have addressed this. We are still addressing it.

Saboteur Four: The 9pm "I Need Water" Phenomenon

It is 9:15pm.

You have completed the routine. You have done the close. You left the room with confidence. You have been sitting quietly for eleven minutes — eleven beautiful, uninterrupted minutes — and you were just starting to believe that tonight was the night it worked.

"Daaaaaad."

"What."

"I need water."

What's actually happening

We'll be brief here because this one is simple: the water request is rarely about water. It is about one more moment of contact before the dark settles in for real. It is the last available card in a hand that has been played down to almost nothing.

This is not cynical. The need behind it is real. The delivery mechanism is just water.

The fix

It is the same fix as every other version of the same problem: **pre-empt it before it becomes a request.**

Water on the nightstand, already there, part of the close. *"Your water is right here."* Said while pointing to the water. Said before they think to ask.

You are not refusing their need. You are meeting it before they have to ask for it, which removes the interaction from the negotiation category entirely. There is nothing to request. The water exists. The need is handled.

Do this for a week and the water requests stop, because the exploit is closed.

The Saboteur Summary

Every saboteur on this list follows the same pattern: **a real need, expressed at a time and in a way that also functions as a delay.** Your child is not usually inventing the fear, the hunger, the thirst. They are real. But they are also, partly, opportunities — gaps in the closing that allow one more moment of connection, light, or parental presence.

The solution is never to dismiss the need. It is to meet the need *inside the routine* before it generates a midnight request. Water on the nightstand. Snack before the sequence. Nightlight chosen and placed. Story ready to play. Alarm clock on the nightstand and phone in the kitchen.

Close the gaps before they find them. They will find every gap you leave open. This is not a criticism — it is an acknowledgment that your children are clever and motivated and you should probably be proud of that even when it is inconvenient.

Now comes the part you've been waiting for.

You have the biology. You have the routines. You've done the self-audit. You know the saboteurs by name.

Chapter 7 is the three-night reset. The specific, sequential, honest plan for what to do starting tonight — or Thursday, if tonight is already gone. What night one looks like. What night two looks like when it's harder than night one. What night three looks like when you're not sure it's working but you're going to hold the line anyway.

And then the cheat sheet. One page. Save it to your phone.

We're almost there.

Chapter 7: The Three-Night Reset — What To Do Starting Tonight →

Chapter 7:

The Three-Night Reset — What To Do Starting Tonight

Let's be honest about something before we start.

You have read six chapters of a book about bedtime. You understand the biology. You recognize yourself in the self-audit. You know the saboteurs by name. You have, at some point in the last hour, thought *yes, this is exactly what's been happening, and I know what to do about it now.*

And there is a version of you — a tired, meeting-tomorrow, boss-is-in-town version of you — who is going to get to night two of this reset and hand someone ice cream and an iPad and think *we'll start again tomorrow.*

We know this because we did it.

Not hypothetically. Specifically. On a real night two, in our real house, with a real critical meeting in the morning and a real boss riding along the next day, George and Julene Gervais — the people who wrote this book about how to fix bedtime — independently, separately, and without consulting each other, arrived at the exact same conclusion:

Not tonight.

George's internal monologue, reconstructed faithfully: *I need sleep tonight. I need to be on my game tomorrow. I cannot do this tonight. We'll start again tomorrow, after the meeting. One night won't matter.*

Julene's internal monologue, happening simultaneously three feet away: *My boss is in town tomorrow. She's riding with me all day. I need my sleep tonight. We'll start fresh tomorrow. One night.*

The ice cream appeared. The iPad was produced. Patrick was released into the night with a vague instruction not to stay up "too long" — a phrase George immediately recognized, even as he said it, as one that required a definition he was not going to provide.

The cheeseburger happened anyway.

In the morning, George looked at Julene across the coffee.

"Try again tonight?"

She nodded.

They drank their coffee. They said nothing else about it all morning. There was no post-mortem. No analysis of what went wrong or whose idea the ice cream was or who had technically authorized Patrick's freedom. Just two people who knew what they'd done, knew what they were going to do instead, and needed caffeine before they could fully commit to it.

That nod is the whole thing.

You don't need a perfect night two. You need a nod across the coffee on the morning after. The reset is not over until you decide it's over.

We are telling you this not because it's funny — though it is — and not because confession is good for the soul — though it is — but because night two is where every reset dies, and it dies for reasons that feel completely legitimate in the moment. You will have a meeting. Your boss will be in town. You will be tired in a way that feels categorically different from regular tired, a tired that seems to justify a one-night exception.

The exception is the trap.

Here is what we learned: the meeting was fine. The boss survived the day. And we spent the next four nights paying the inconsistency tax on the two nights we gave away on ice cream and good intentions.

One night does matter. Not catastrophically. Not permanently. But it matters.

Read this chapter before night two. Remember this story on night two. Then do the thing anyway.

Before You Start: The Setup Night

The three-night reset doesn't begin on night one. It begins the afternoon before night one, with a conversation.

Not a lecture. Not a rules announcement. A conversation — calm, matter-of-fact, at a neutral time when nobody is tired and nobody is already in a standoff. Dinner table. Car ride. After school. Wherever your family talks.

The script is simple:

"Hey — we're going to try something new at bedtime starting tonight. Here's what it's going to look like."

Then walk through the routine. Briefly. Specifically. Tell them what time the sequence starts, what the sequence is, what the close looks like, and what happens if they get out of bed. No drama. No threat energy. The energy of someone announcing a schedule change, not declaring war.

For the older kids and teens, explain the why. Use the biology from Chapter 2. Show Patrick his Garmin data if you have it. Tell him you're not doing this to be difficult — you're doing it because you've been watching him run on not enough sleep for too long and you're changing that, starting tonight.

For the little ones, make it slightly exciting. New routine. New nightlight if you're getting one. New closing ritual if you're building one. Kids this age respond well to novelty inside structure — the new thing that then becomes the same thing every night.

Then do it. Tonight. Not Thursday. Not after the weekend. Tonight.

Night One: Plant the Flag

Night one of a reset is usually not the hardest night. Night one has novelty on its side. Everyone knows something is different. You have energy and intention. The conversation happened. You are ready.

Here is what night one looks like, step by step, for each age group.

Night One: Little Ones (Ages 2–5)

5:45pm — If your target sleep time is 7:00, you are starting dinner no later than 5:30. This is the part most parents skip and then wonder why the routine is rushed. Everything downstream of a late dinner is compressed and stressed.

6:30pm — Transition warning. *"Thirty minutes until bath time."* Not a negotiation. An announcement. Said cheerfully.

7:00pm — Routine starts. Bath or wash-up. Pajamas. Teeth. One book. Closing ritual. Water on the nightstand. Bridge object in position.

7:25pm — Lights out. Check-in promised for five minutes. *"I'll be back to check on you in five minutes. Everything you need is right here."*

7:30pm — Check-in. Brief. Boring. *"Just checking. You good? Okay. Goodnight."* Leave.

What will happen: At least one callback. Possibly several. You return once — warmly, briefly, boringly — and then you hold the line. The callback is not an emergency. It is a test. Your job is to be the least interesting thing that has happened all day.

What success looks like on night one: Asleep by 7:45 or 8:00. Maybe one or two callbacks that you handled without caving. The routine completed. The flag planted.

Night One: School Age (Ages 6–10)

7:00pm — Screens off. This is the moment. Hold it with the calm certainty of someone who has read the science and made a decision. Device goes to the designated charging spot. Not their room. Done.

7:00–7:30pm — Wind-down activity. Book, drawing, puzzle. In their room or in a quiet space. You are not supervising — you are available.

7:30pm — Hygiene. Teeth, face, whatever your standard is. Independent. Verified once.

7:40pm — Check-in conversation. Sit on the edge of the bed. One real question. Five to ten minutes. Then the close.

8:00pm — Lights out. Warm, final, no-lingering close. Water on nightstand. *"Goodnight. I love you. See you in the morning."* Leave.

What will happen: There will be a callback. Possibly the water request, even though the water is right there. Possibly a suddenly-remembered homework item. Possibly nothing — night one sometimes goes surprisingly smoothly because the novelty holds.

What success looks like on night one: Asleep by 8:20 or 8:30. The screen cutoff held. The close was final. You didn't re-enter more than once.

Night One: Tweens and Teens (Ages 11–13)

8:30pm — Phone handoff. This is the line. The alarm clock is already on the nightstand — you set it up this afternoon, before this conversation happened, so the alarm clock objection is already closed. The phone goes to the kitchen charging station. Yours too.

"But I was just—"

"I know. Phones are charging. See you in a bit."

Said with the breezy confidence of someone who has already decided and is not reopening the discussion.

8:30–9:30pm — Wind-down block. Their choice of screenless activity. Music is fine. A book. A journal. Whatever they'll actually do. You've given them the block and the parameters. Step back.

9:45pm — Knock. Head in the door. *"You good?"* Low-key. Genuine. Brief. Close with warmth and leave without hovering.

10:00pm — Lights out.

What will happen: Resistance at the phone handoff. Possibly significant resistance. Hold the line with low drama — not a fight, not a negotiation, just a calm and final non-event. The goal is to make the handoff so boring and inevitable that there's nothing to push against.

What success looks like on night one: Phone in the kitchen. Lights out by 10:00 or 10:15. No cheeseburger. No milkshake. You wake up in the morning with your sleep score intact and Patrick in his room.

Night Two: The Hard Night

Night two is harder than night one. We have told you this. We are telling you again because knowing it in the abstract is different from feeling it at 8:45pm when you are depleted and the resistance is higher than last night and some part of your brain is quietly suggesting that the ice cream is right there in the freezer.

Here is why night two is harder:

On night one, the novelty held. Everyone knew something was different. The conversation had just happened. The energy was fresh.

On night two, the novelty is gone. What remains is the reality of the new routine, which your child has now assessed overnight and concluded is not in their interest. The resistance on night two is more deliberate, more targeted, and more likely to find the exact pressure point that makes you fold — because they've had twenty-four hours to identify it.

For the little ones, night two often brings bigger tears and more emotional escalation. They've confirmed the new thing is real and they want you to know they don't like it.

For the school-age kid, night two brings the most creative objections. The homework that needs discussing. The feelings about something that happened at school two weeks ago that are suddenly urgent. The theological questions about death that cannot wait until morning.

For Patrick, night two brings the full diplomatic arsenal. The reasoned argument. The appeal to fairness. The comparison to what other kids' parents allow. Delivered, possibly, with the kind of calm, logical energy that makes you briefly wonder if he has a point.

He does not have a point. He has a very good argument, which is a different thing.

How to survive night two

Before the routine starts: Remind yourself of the inconsistency tax. Every night you give away, you pay for on the next two or three. The meeting is not a reason to cave. The boss riding along is not a reason to cave. Those things are real and they are hard and they are also not related to whether your child's bedtime happens tonight. Your tiredness is real. It is also not a reason to cave. You were tired last night too. You will be tired tomorrow.

During the routine: Do everything slower and calmer than last night. The instinct on a hard night is to rush — to push through the resistance with urgency. Urgency raises cortisol, which raises the temperature of everything, which makes sleep harder for everyone. Slow down. Do the routine at the pace of someone who has nowhere to be and nothing to prove.

At the moment of maximum resistance — the tears, the argument, the ice cream temptation — say this to yourself: *night three is easier. I just have to get to night three.*

Because night three is easier. Not easy. Easier. And night four is easier than that. And by night seven, you are living in a different house than the one you were in last week.

If you cave on night two: Don't quit the reset. Acknowledge it, without drama, and start again the next night. Not from zero — you've already planted the flag, done night one, learned something. One cave doesn't erase that. What erases it is deciding the reset is over because you had a hard night.

The reset is not over. Start again tomorrow. Leave the ice cream in the freezer this time.

Night Three: The Turn

Something shifts on night three.

Not dramatically. Not in a way that feels like victory. It feels more like — less. Less resistance at the phone handoff. Fewer callbacks. The little one who was sobbing on night two goes through the closing ritual on night three with something approaching resignation, which in toddler terms is basically consent.

The resistance isn't gone. But it's lost some of its conviction. Your child is beginning — just beginning — to encode the new sequence as the thing that happens now. The testing is becoming perfunctory rather than genuine.

You will be tempted to interpret this as success and loosen something. Don't. Night three is not the finish line. It is the first indication that you are building something real. Hold every piece of the routine exactly as you held it on nights one and two.

Night three for little ones:

The callbacks will be fewer. Honor the check-in anyway. Do the closing ritual anyway, with the same words in the same order. The consistency is the point. You are not just trying to get them to sleep tonight — you are wiring a sequence that will run on autopilot by night fourteen.

Night three for school age:

The screen cutoff is starting to feel like a fact rather than a fight. The wind-down activity is becoming the thing they just do. The check-in conversation may go longer tonight — something may surface that didn't come up on nights one or two, now that the routine feels safer. Let it. This is the routine working.

Night three for tweens and teens:

This is the night Patrick might say something that surprises you. It won't be *"you were right about the phone."* Thirteen-year-olds do not say that. It will be something smaller — a detail about his day offered unprompted during the check-in, or the absence of a fight at the phone handoff that you notice only because you were braced for one.

Notice it. Don't make a big deal of it. Just notice it.

Nights Four Through Fourteen: The Build

We won't script these night by night because by night four the routine should be running well enough that you don't need a script. What you need is a commitment: fourteen nights before you evaluate whether it's working.

Not seven. Not ten. Fourteen.

By night fourteen, one of three things will be true:

The routine is working. Bedtime is smoother, faster, and lower-conflict than it was two weeks ago. Your child is getting more sleep. You are getting more evening. The war is not over, but the daily battles are shorter and the outcomes are more predictable. This is the most likely result if you held the routine consistently.

The routine is mostly working with one persistent problem. A specific saboteur that didn't close. A callback loop that's down to one but not zero. A teen who is doing the phone handoff but pushing the lights-out time. These are fixable and specific — go back to the relevant chapter and tighten the one piece that isn't holding.

The routine isn't working and you're not sure why. This is less common but it happens. If you've held the routine consistently for fourteen nights and things are not improving, there may be something else going on — a sleep disorder, an anxiety issue that goes beyond normal bedtime fear, something happening at school or socially that is disrupting sleep from the inside. This book is not a substitute for a pediatrician or a child psychologist if something deeper is at play. Trust your instincts. If something feels like more than a bedtime problem, it might be.

The One-Paragraph Version of This Entire Chapter

Pick your age-appropriate routine from Chapter 4. Do it tonight. Do it again tomorrow night even though tomorrow night is harder. Do it again on night three even though you're not sure it's working. Do it for fourteen nights before you decide anything. Don't give away ice cream on night two. Get the alarm clock before the conversation about the phone. Hold every piece of the routine with the calm certainty of someone who has read the science and made a decision.

That's it. That's the reset.

One chapter left. The cheat sheet — one page, everything you need, save it to your phone and never read this book again unless you want to.

You're almost there.

Chapter 8: The Cheat Sheet →

Chapter 8:

The Cheat Sheet

You made it.

What follows is a recap of everything in this book — the biology, the routines by age, the saboteurs, the reset — distilled into one chapter you can return to any time you need it.

And here's what we really want you to have.

Go to
HowToGetYourKidsToGotoBed.com
and download the free
Bedtime Battle Cheat Sheet.

It's everything in this chapter — plus the exact words to use when things go sideways, the top mistakes to stop making tonight, and the three sentences that will get you through any bedtime. One designed page. Ready to print, stick on the fridge, save to your phone, or slide across the counter to your partner without saying a word. You earned it. And you'll be really glad you have it the next time bedtime turns into a battle.

Now let's make sure you're ready.

THE BIOLOGY IN THREE SENTENCES

Your child's brain needs two things to fall asleep: a full adenosine tank (built all day, drained by sugar and caffeine) and a rising melatonin signal (blocked by every screen in your house). Stress and conflict raise cortisol, which fights both. Your teenager's clock has shifted one to three hours later — this is biology, not attitude.

BY AGE: THE ESSENTIALS

LITTLE ONES — Ages 2–5

How much sleep: 11–13 hours **Target lights-out:** 7:00–7:30pm **Start routine:** 6:30pm

The routine:

1. Transition warning — *"Five minutes to bath time"*
2. Bath or warm wash-up
3. Pajamas + teeth — same order, every night
4. One book — same book is fine, boring is good

5. Closing ritual — song, prayer, three gratitudes, whatever — identical every night
6. Pre-empt — *"Water's here. [Stuffed animal] is here. Anything else before lights out?"*
7. Lights out + check-in promised — *"I'll check on you in five minutes"*
8. Five-minute check-in — brief, boring, final

Top saboteurs:

- Missed sleep window → overtiredness looks like energy
- Separation anxiety → met with presence, not distance
- The callback loop → closed by the pre-empt + promised check-in

Remember: The sequence is the signal. Same order, every night, for fourteen nights. The brain learns to start shutting down when the sequence begins.

SCHOOL AGE — Ages 6–10

How much sleep: 9–11 hours **Target lights-out:** 8:00–8:30pm **Start routine:** 7:00pm

The routine:

1. Screens off — devices to charging station, not their room
2. Wind-down activity — reading, drawing, puzzle — 20–30 minutes
3. Hygiene — independent, verified once
4. Check-in conversation — one real question, 5–10 minutes
5. Close — warm, final, no-lingering — *"Goodnight. I love you. See you in the morning."*
6. Hold the line — callbacks met with boring, loving, one-time response

Top saboteurs:

- Screens in the last hour → melatonin suppressed, sleep delayed
- The negotiation trap → bedtime is an announcement, not an opening offer
- The homework ambush → homework before wind-down, non-negotiable

Remember: Work backwards from wake time. Subtract ten hours. That's your lights-out target. Most parents work forwards from dinner and wonder why it's always late.

TWEENS + EARLY TEENS — Ages 11–13

How much sleep: 8–10 hours **Target lights-out:** 10:00–10:30pm **Start routine:** 8:30pm

The routine:

1. Phone to kitchen charging station — yours too — alarm clock already on nightstand
2. Wind-down block — their choice of screenless activity — 60 minutes
3. Hygiene — their responsibility, one non-nagging check
4. Optional check-in — knock, head in, one low-stakes question
5. Close — *"Goodnight, love you"* — warm, brief, not weird

Top saboteurs:

- Phone in the room → single highest-impact sleep destroyer for this age

- The alarm clock defense → solve it before the conversation with a $9 alarm clock
- Treating teen sleep like little-kid sleep → different biology, different approach

Remember: Show them their own data. A thirteen-year-old who can see the correlation between their sleep score and their performance is more persuadable than one who is just being told what to do.

THE SELF-AUDIT: STOP DOING THESE

- ❌ Agreeing to "five more minutes"
- ❌ Offering rewards mid-standoff
- ❌ The re-tuck, more than once
- ❌ Screens in the last hour before bed
- ❌ Checking your own phone while telling them to put theirs down
- ❌ Skipping the routine because the night is already a write-off
- ❌ Threats you won't follow through on

THE THREE-NIGHT RESET

Setup afternoon: Have the conversation. Calm, specific, no drama. *"Here's what bedtime looks like starting tonight."* Buy the alarm clock before the phone conversation.

Night one: Plant the flag. Do the full routine. Hold the close. Handle callbacks with boring, loving finality. Success = routine completed, not perfection.

Night two: The hard night. Resistance will be higher. Your meeting is not a reason to cave. The ice cream is not a solution. Say to yourself: *night three is easier. I just have to get to night three.* If you cave — start again tomorrow. The reset is not over.

Night three: Something shifts. Less resistance. More resignation. Hold every piece of the routine anyway. You are not at the finish line — you are at the first sign that something is being built.

Nights four through fourteen: Same routine. Every night. No evaluation until night fourteen. By then, one of three things is true: it's working, one piece needs fixing, or something deeper is going on and it's time to call the pediatrician.

THE THREE SENTENCES TO MEMORIZE

"Bedtime isn't a negotiation. It's a sequence."

"You are not just trying to get through tonight. You are building something."

"Night three is easier. Just get to night three."

The Quick Snapshot

	Ages 2-5	Ages 6-10	Ages 11-13
Sleep needed	11-13 hours	9-11 hours	8-10 hours
Lights out	7:00-7:30pm	8:00-8:30pm	10:00-10:30pm
Routine starts	6:30pm	7:00pm	8:30pm
Biggest saboteur	Missed window	Screens & Negotiation	Phone in room
Key move	Same sequence nightly	Hard screen cutoff	Phone to kitchen
Reset takes	14 nights	14 nights	14 nights

ONE LAST THING

You are a good parent. You are a tired parent. These are not contradictory. Every mistake in this book — the ice cream, the re-tuck, the iPad deal, the night two cave — happened in our house, to us, on real nights when we were doing our best with what we had.

The goal is not a perfect bedtime. The goal is a better one. One that's a little calmer, a little earlier, and a little more predictable than the one you had before you read this.

Your kid can sleep.

You can get there.

Start tonight.

— George & Julene, Authors and Parents just like you.

HowToGetYourKidsToGotoBed.com

APPENDIX: The Economics of Bedtime

Or: What the Cheeseburger Actually Costs

We have spent this entire book being honest about our own failures — the ice cream in bed, the pretending to be asleep, the 1:30am kitchen situation we will not relitigate here. We have been funny about it because some of it genuinely deserves humor.

This part does not.

If you are the kind of parent who needs the research before you fully commit to a sleep system, this appendix is for you. The data is real, the sources are cited, and the math is straightforward.

Close your eyes for one second before you read further.

Picture your child's face.

Now keep reading.

What sleep actually does to a developing brain

Sleep is not downtime. It is the period during which your child's brain consolidates what it learned during the day — transferring information from short-term to long-term memory, clearing metabolic waste, and rebuilding the capacity for focus and decision-making that the next school day will require.

Dr. Mary Carskadon at Brown University has spent decades documenting what happens to adolescent cognition under chronic sleep restriction. The finding is consistent: reaction time degrades, working memory shrinks, and the prefrontal cortex — the part of the brain responsible for planning, focus, and impulse control — is disproportionately affected by sleep loss compared to every other brain region.

A 2006 review by Curcio, Ferrara, and De Gennaro in Sleep Medicine Reviews synthesized decades of research connecting sleep loss to academic performance. Children and adolescents with insufficient or irregular sleep demonstrate meaningfully lower academic performance than their well-rested peers. Not slightly lower. Consistently, measurably, significantly lower.

Think about your child's last big test. Their last school project. The morning they walked in exhausted versus the morning they walked in rested. You already know the difference. You have seen it on their face at the breakfast table.

How many nights between now and graduation?

If your child is nine years old, the answer is roughly 3,300. Each one is either working for them or against them. There is no neutral night.

What the Bureau of Labor Statistics says

Academic performance affects education attainment. Education attainment affects lifetime earnings. The Bureau of Labor Statistics publishes this data every year, and the numbers are not subtle.

The following figures come from the BLS Education Pays 2023 report, adjusted to approximate 2026 dollars using the Consumer Price Index. A note on the numbers: "median weekly earnings" means that if you lined up every working adult in America from the lowest-paid to the highest-paid, the person standing exactly in the middle earns this much per week. Half of all workers earn more. Half earn less. It is the most honest single number for what a job actually pays in real life.

(Data from the Bureau of Labor Statistics table is on the next page)

Data from the Bureau of Labor Statistics Education Pays report (*adjusted for 2026*)		
Education Level	**Median weekly earnings (2026 est)**	**Estimated 40yr career earnings**
Less than high school diploma	$682	$1.4M
High school diploma	$882	$1.8M
Some college, no degree	$1,019	$2.1M
Associate's degree	$1,092	$2.3M
Bachelor's degree	$1,561	$3.2M
Master's degree	$1,893	$3.9M

Source: U.S. Bureau of Labor Statistics, Education Pays 2023. Figures adjusted to approximate 2026 dollars using BLS Consumer Price Index data. Career earnings calculated as median weekly earnings × 52 weeks × 40 working years.

The gap between a high school diploma and a bachelor's degree is approximately $1.4 million over a working lifetime. Before investment returns. Before promotions. Before the compounding effect of showing up, for forty years, as someone whose brain was built on a foundation of actual sleep.

Now ask yourself the question most parents never think to ask:

What does your child want to be when they grow up?

Whatever they said — the doctor, the engineer, the artist, the athlete, the person who owns their own business someday — sleep is part of the infrastructure that gets them there. Not the only part. Not a guarantee. But a foundation that everything else gets built on top of.

What is being built in your house right now, tonight, while the screens are still on?

The gap nobody sees coming

We are not saying bedtime is the only variable. We are not saying a child who goes to bed on time is guaranteed any particular outcome. Parenting is not a formula and life is not a spreadsheet.

What we are saying is this: sleep is one of the most consistent, most studied, and most actionable levers available to a parent of a school-age child. It costs nothing. It requires no special equipment, no tutoring, no expensive program. It requires a system, some consistency, and the willingness to hold the line on the nights it is inconvenient.

The parents who hold that line are not doing it because bedtime is fun. They are doing it because they have made a quiet decision about what they want for their child's future — and they have connected that future to what happens in their house at 8pm.

Have you made that decision yet?

If you are reading this appendix, we think you have. Or you are very close.

The prime rib scenario

The cheeseburger is funny. It will always be funny.

But picture your child at twenty-five. Thirty-five. At the age you are right now, looking back at the foundation they were given and what they built on top of it.

The version of your child who slept — who consolidated what they learned, who woke up with their prefrontal cortex restored, who did this not just tonight but across the years when their brain was doing its most important developmental work — that version of your child is building something real.

The cheeseburger is fine.

You want prime rib for them.

That is what this book is for. And tonight is a very good place to start.

Sources

Bureau of Labor Statistics, U.S. Department of Labor. Education Pays, 2023. bls.gov/emp/chart-unemployment-earnings-education.htm

Carskadon, Mary A. "Sleep's Effects on Cognition and Learning in Adolescence." Progress in Brain Research, 2011.

Curcio, G., Ferrara, M., and De Gennaro, L. "Sleep loss, learning capacity and academic performance." Sleep Medicine Reviews, 2006.

Czeisler, C.A. et al. "Exposure to room light before bedtime suppresses melatonin onset." Journal of Clinical Endocrinology & Metabolism, 2011.

National Sleep Foundation. "Sleep in America Poll: Sleep and Technology." sleepfoundation.org

About the Authors

George and Julene Gervais are the parents of three children — ages nine, fourteen, and twenty-one — and the authors of this book. They live in North Yarmouth, Maine, where bedtime has been, at various points, a negotiation, a disaster, and eventually a system that actually works.

George is the founder of Focus On It, LLC, The Harmonic Advantage, GetTheGiftNow.com, and a few other ideas as he lets his creative side out to play with his entrepreneurial self. He is a thirty-year entrepreneur, a former member of Maine's Governor's cabinet, and occasional author. He is also a passionate musician, playing five different instruments, and once owned and operated three restaurants. None of this prepared him for the 1:30am cheeseburger situation.

Julene is a two-time President's Club Sales Professional, a former CBS television news anchor and reporter, and the producer and host of *Greenlight Maine.* She is also the co-founder of JulesandNini.com, and co-founded MissionJunes.com alongside her husband and a partner. She spent twenty years learning how to talk to people who don't want to hear what she's saying. This skill transfers directly to parenting.

They wrote this book because the version that would have helped them didn't exist yet.

Watch for **More from**
the HowToGetYourFamily Series

How To Get Your Kids To Brush Their Teeth —
The Manual

How To Get Your Kids To Clean Their Room —
The Manual

How To Get Your Kids Off Their Phone —
The Manual

How To Get Your Husband
To Do Anything You Want
— The Ultimate Manual

HowToGetYourFamilyToDoStuff.com

www.ingramcontent.com/pod-product-compliance
Lightning Source LLC
LaVergne TN
LVHW010605160826
845677LV00013B/3253

9798992788440